The Revolutionary Leadership

LANCASTER COUNTY DURING THE AMERICAN REVOLUTION

Joseph E. Walker, Editor

The Revolutionary Leadership

by

G. Terry Madonna

Original Illustrations by Henry M. Libhart

Lancaster

A BICENTENNIAL BOOK

1976

The Revolutionary Leadership ISBN 0-915010-07-0

Copyright © 1976 by Lancaster County Historical Society.

Printed in the United States of America.

Library of Congress Catalog Card No. 76-8955

A BICENTENNIAL BOOK *published by*
LANCASTER COUNTY BICENTENNIAL COMMITTEE, INC.
Co-published and distributed by
Sutter House
Box 146, Lititz, Pa. 17543

Foreword

Since the inception of the Lancaster County Bicentennial Committee, its stated major objective has been the involvement of the individual in the preservation of his own rich heritage. We hope to restate the obvious; to discover again things long since set aside or forgotten; to identify that which has been overlooked or has taken on new meaning during these past 200 years.

This book and the series of which it is a part are some of the fruits of that objective. Perhaps it will serve as the inspiration to explore the past and as a guide to make the jorney more rewarding,

DONALD G. GOLDSTROM

Introduction

Officers and soldiers receive most of the attention in the chronicles of war. But back on the home front there are men and women who are entrusted with the unglamorous tasks of seeing that life goes on and that supplies keep moving to the front.

Revolutions have need for yet other kinds of leaders—the philosopher, the idealist, the pamphleteer, the orator. These are the framers of issues, the originators of causes, the creators of enthusiasm, the whippers of flagging spirits. They push for a resolution of injustices "be it war itself." They state the grounds for the conflict. They sustain the cause when lesser zealots tire of the labor, the cost, the bloodshed.

Dr. G. Terry Madonna has traced the careers of twelve such men who labored to present the American cause against British taxes to the people of Lancaster County. They wrote ringing declarations of liberty and independence. They organized local committees. They served in state and national legislative assemblies. Some were in the army for a part of the war, but their services as intellectuals in the cause of freedom were of more significance.

Professor Henry M. Libhart of Elizabethtown College has provided the visual representation of this political leadership in ten illustrations.

This book is the fifth in a series depicting phases of the Revolution in Lancaster County. Previous titles were: *A Way of Life, The Pennsylvania Rifle, Fighting the Battles* and *The Perils of Patriotism.* Forthcoming volumes will tell of the service of supply and of the problems of those who objected to war—or to this war.

THE EDITOR

Preface

More than two hundred years ago a revolution unlike any in world history broke out in the British colonies in North America. Nor has any revolutionary struggle since been quite like the American Revolution. Recorders of these events have paid special attention to its leaders: especially men like Samuel and John Adams of Massachusetts; George Washington, Patrick Henry and Thomas Jefferson of Virginia; and Alexander Hamilton and John Jay of New York. Pennsylvanians such as Benjamin Franklin, John Dickinson and Joseph Galloway have also received lavish treatment.

Yet, in William Penn's colony in Lancaster County, there emerged a group of revolutionaries highly sensitive to the issues of the day, and sufficiently motivated by them to rebel. This slender volume attempts to chronicle the role played by Lancaster's major political leaders during the Revolution. To be sure, it is not a complete account, but it tries to describe who the leaders were, why they participated and in what manner. It is not a military history and neither deals with the battles nor the figures involved in military operations. Where overlap exists between military affairs and political leadership, the emphasis is on the latter.

THE DAY A REVOLUTION WAS MADE

The Conservative Patriot

*G*EORGE ROSS WHEELED HIS HORSE around on a muggy May 1, 1775, and began the short ride from his country estate to the Grape Tavern. As Ross moved slowly southward towards the center of the borough, his thoughts wandered to the alarming news that had reached Lancaster the previous week—news that now required his present ride. The announcement of the fighting at Lexington and Concord between British regulars and a ragtag assortment of patriot farmers and villagers, with the loss of lives on both sides, had arrived with the fury and abandon of a sage brush fire, consuming all in its path. The entire county raged with excitement, and cries for armed resistance circulated widely.

Ross, who had been in Philadelphia with the General Assembly, returned to Lancaster, for he was the central figure among the local patriots. In Philadelphia he had heard many conflicting reports about the fighting, but the consequences of the military engagements seemed crystal clear. The British had to be resisted forcibly. Ross was convinced that armed resistance remained the only feasible course of action open. Lexington and Concord left no doubt about that.

Ironically, although Ross had become a revolutionary, he did not feel like one. His social views were quite conservative, and he could only believe that the current struggle involved the preservation of liberties that Americans already had as colonials. The prospect of war with Great Britain sent cold chills along Ross's spine as he rode his horse along dusty Queen Street. Yet, living under a crown that oppressed colonial rights and a Parliament that taxed people without their consent was even a less appealing prospect.

Ross had slipped into his revolutionary role gradually, though decisively, as events in the 1770's pressed Americans everywhere into overt action. The events in Boston triggered the latest crisis. Radical patriots under the direction of Sam Adams had dumped a large quantity of British tea into Boston harbor. The British Parliament responded by closing the harbor, by removing a substantial number of jury trials out of Boston, and by revising the Massachusetts colonial charter, thereby depriving the colony of long-standing political liberties.

The tough British response caused a tremendous reaction in Lancaster, where, amidst calls for an immediate response, a large group met on June 15, 1774 in the court house. The meeting was led by Lancaster's most influential and wealthy citizens, including Ross, Edward Shippen, Jasper Yeates, Matthias Slough, James Webb, William Henry, William Bausman and Charles Hall. Where they would lead, most others would follow.

This incipient group of revolutionaries elected a Committee of Correspondence to keep countians informed of the latest developments and then issued a series of provocative resolutions in defense of colonial rights, especially condemning the closing of Boston harbor. The local patriots stated their support for a total boycott of British goods and were prepared to apply some pressure to county merchants should they not comply. Most merchants did, however.

For Ross the summer of 1774 proved critical. Flushed with their initial success, the local patriots held a second meeting in early July with a much larger attendance. Ross chaired the meeting, but the real decisions had been reached privately by the coterie of prominent men who had started the earlier one. Yet Ross made the public address that day and, in fact, was more identified publicly with the patriot cause than anyone else. Although he expressed total loyalty to "his most gracious majesty King George," Ross declared the Boston action of the British Government to be "unconstitutional, unjust and oppressive." He further emphasized, and the group enthusiastically approved, local support for the calling of a continental congress, in

Sign of the White Swan Tavern, located on the southeast corner of Penn Square and Queen Street.

effect a union of all the colonies. There could be no doubt that the local patriot endorsement of a general congress was a radical act, one that put Ross into the vanguard of the revolutionary movement.

While serving in the Pennsylvania Assembly that summer, Ross continued to champion the cause of the congress. So pronounced was his advocacy that, when it was finally authorized, he became one of Pennsylvania's delegates.

The Ageless Revolutionary

During the summer of 1774, a second major activity occupied the attention of local patriots. As a consequence of British policy, momentary economic hardship befell the normally prosperous seacoast town of Boston. Lancasterians busily organized a relief effort. The task fell to Ross's friend and the patriarch of Lancaster patriots, Edward Shippen, who, though in his 70's, was a tireless organizer. If Ross was the actual spearhead of the local revolutionary movement, Shippen, by virtue of his age, background and influence, was its titular leader. Deeply disturbed, however, by British policies, Shippen assumed actual command of the drive for Boston relief funds.

By September 154 pounds had been collected from sympathizers in all parts of the county. Donations poured in from men and women alike; from the rich and the not-so-rich and from people of every religious and ethnic background. Organizing the Boston relief was not the first occasion that had caused Shippen to have doubts about the nature of British rule.

In his early years in Lancaster, Shippen centered his attention on the import-export business, establishing a thriving trade with the Indians. This trade was all-inclusive, involving everything from thread, gunpowder, silk hose, guns and hats, to rum, lead, flints, kettles and knives. After the French and Indian War in 1763, the Indian trade was somewhat curtailed by customarily bad economic times that normally follow wars, and by the taxation policies of the British government, especially as prices fell. Then, too, an incessant period of Indian fighting further complicated the economic picture.

Since most of the new tax policies involved duties on imports, Shippen developed an intense hostility towards them. He eagerly supported the boycott of imported British goods. His opposition stemmed not only from personal loss but from firm conviction that the policies themselves were "unconstitutional and oppressive." This attitude was widely held in Lancaster, because in 1770 local patriots, following a public demonstration, made known their intention to seize any British goods brought into the county in violation of a temporarily established boycott. Indeed, violators were subjected to intimidation and threat and considered "traitors to the true interest of the country."

If such talk seemed tough, it stemmed from the realization that the British government had never attempted to raise a revenue in colonies and was now vigorously doing just that. Shippen's opposition focused on the much-hated Stamp Act of 1765 which taxed virtually every type of printed matter. It was a bothersome and expensive interference with business. He singled it out for special castigation, claiming that no one could conceive of a "more offensive act." The fact that British merchants reaped a profit of slightly less than two million pounds a year merely compounded the problem. Shippen likened the profit advantage to the "old woman who killed her hen who laid but one golden egg a day in hopes of finding millions in her body."

Thus, Shippen had become, by May 1, 1775, an ardent revolutionary. He, too, would attend the Grape Tavern meeting and, like Ross, was quite prepared to accept the consequences of his action.

The Faithful Supplier

While Ross continued his ride toward the center of the borough, Matthias Slough was preparing to walk the hundred yards from his own tavern, the White Swan, situated on the square, to the Grape. Before departing, however, the tavernkeeper peered into an adjacent storeroom and observed that a sizeable quantity of gunpowder and lead was on hand. Requests for such valuable materials had already been made, and Slough had decided to place this stock at the disposal of the Revolutionary forces. In fact, in the succeeding years, he would make large quantities of all kinds of provisions available to the Continental Army.

Slough was more than willing to do what he viewed as his proper duty, even though he had seen more than his share of violence and death, and the prospect of war promised to offer more of the same. As coroner, he had witnessed the atrocities committed by white man upon Indian, and Indian upon white man in the 1750's and 1760's, culminating in the massacre of several peaceful Conestoga Indians by the so-called Paxton Boys. The inhabitants of Lancaster, since its founding, had been exposed to Indian attack, especially the residents of its northern townships, Paxton and Donegal. Lancaster was still very much part of the frontier, and the threat of Indian danger would be increased as a result of the war with England. The tavern owner was disturbed by this fact, but he was prepared to accept it as a result of the much longer struggle.

The Radical Inn-Keeper

A second tavern keeper had spent this particular May 1st preparing for the arrival of his guests. Adam Reigart glanced around the Grape Tavern's main dining room and saw that it was filling to capacity. George Ross had arrived and stood huddling with Edward Shippen. Most of the other patriot leaders had also arrived—William Atlee, William Bausman, Charles Hall, Casper Schaffner, William Henry and Samuel Bare.

Although the large crowd would tax the Grape's physical capacity, Reigart was not the least concerned with such mundane matters. For days, since the news of Lexington and Concord, the Tavern had bustled with tremendous activity as visitors came and went inquiring about the latest news from Massachusetts. Reigart was now accustomed to both the increased business and the break with normal routine. In fact, these events realized Reigart's fondest expectations, and the tavern keeper, long Lancaster's most radical agitator, viewed them as the culmination of a personal struggle. The radicalism of Reigart brought the obvious comparison with Samuel Adams, the Massachusetts firebrand and revolutionary agitator and organizer.

In the months following the tea act crisis, local patriots, spurred on by Reigart, had been meeting in the latter's home. These meetings occurred infrequently, yet the borough's Committee of Observation had met privately, and plans for complying with the directives of the First Continental Congress were made. Many lengthy discussions regarding the nature of the conflict between the colonies and Great Britain had a salutary effect in bringing the doubtfuls among Lancaster's political leaders around to a more radical position. The most important meeting was held on April 27, 1775, just three days before the patriots assembled at the Grape, and plans were laid for the forthcoming public meeting. Post riders circulated news of the meeting throughout the county, thereby insuring a large crowd.

Interestingly, the Grape became the favorite rendezvous and general headquarters for patriots, especially in the April to August 1775 period. Reigart, a man of considerable wealth, owned several

Sign of the Grape Tavern, located on North Queen Street.

other taverns which were also centers of revolutionary activity. These other hostelries served as communication and organization centers, and, since the county in 1775 was twice its present size, they took on an added dimension.

The Patriot Attorney

A block away, in his law office, Jasper Yeates made a last minute check of the resolutions that would be submitted momentarily to the patriot assembly at the Grape. Stacks of handbills were piled in a corner where printer Francis Bailey had deposited them, and Yeates told his law clerk to carry them to the Grape. Yeates' eyes scanned the resolutions that appeared on the handbills; the words fairly leaped off the paper,

> Whereas, the enemies of Great Britain and America have resolved by force of arms to carry into execution the most unjust, tyrannical, and cruel edicts of the British Parliament, and reduced freeborn sons of America to a state of vassalage, and have flattered themselves, from our unacquaintance with military discipline, that we should become an easy prey to them, or tamely submit and bend our necks to the yoke prepared for us: we do most solemnly agree and associate under the deepest sense of our duty to God, our country, ourselves and posterity, to defend and protect the religious and civil rights of this and our sister colonies, with our lives and fortunes . . .

Other resolutions went on to call for the establishment of militia companies and the election of military officers. Yeates understood well that these resolutions were treasonous; that local patriots were perhaps burning the last bridge between themselves and the Mother Country by publicly approving these resolutions.

The statement, with precision and decisiveness, was a clarion call to resist the policies of the British Government by force, even though the colonists admitted a certain lack of knowledge regarding military affairs. The agreement to "associate" was especially pregnant with consequences. Less than a week after the Grape meeting, patriot leaders began a census of the entire county, and white males between the ages of 16–50 were expected to "volunteer" for military duty. A second activity revolved around the collection of military supplies. The Committee of Observation was empowered to search local stores to determine what quantity of powder and lead was available, and

The pipe box was a convenience adding to the pleasure of many of the inn's customers. The clay pipes, mostly imported, were generally "on the house."

store-keepers were expressly forbidden to sell these products, unless they obtained a license from the committee. In short, support of the Revolution was no longer a matter of individual conscience or decision. Patriot leaders were prepared to force all countains to submit to their newly adopted policies.

Edward Shippen read the resolutions slowly, carefully enunciating each word. Complete silence enveloped the Grape during the brief proceeding. It was shortly after 2:00 P.M., yet scores of farmers and workmen crowded the Grape's courtyard. Following the formal reading, the resolutions were approved unanimously. A great cheer went up, and the crowd dispersed. As Ross began the ride home, he realized that the decisions just ratified marked the beginning, not the end, of what promised to be a lengthy struggle. But these were men who were prepared to risk revolution, confident that freedom and liberty could be preserved. Too, they were men who were future-oriented, convinced, in George Washington's words, that "with our fate will the destiny of unborn millions be involved." Lastly, they realized that, although destiny was being determined by them, no one was going to show them the way. Ross would have certainly agreed with James Madison when the latter said, "We are in a wilderness without a single footstep to guide us. Our successors will have an easier task."

State Leadership

Patriot leaders in Lancaster county also participated in the popular uprising against England on a colony-wide basis. In this capacity they, along with ardent patriots elsewhere, constituted a crucial element in swinging Pennsylvania toward a strong line of resistance. In June 1774 the British government closed the port of Boston, and that summer marked the beginning of noticeable colony-wide leadership from Lancaster County. Radical patriots in Pennsylvania were supporting the proposed Continental Congress.

Although the Lancaster County delegation was solidly for the proposal, the Pennsylvania Assembly contained many representatives who were opposed to it. Patriot leaders in Philadelphia, determined to see the colony represented in the Congress, issued a call for a colony-wide Convention, which it was believed would represent the sovereign will of the people. This decision was definitely revolutionary because,

Sign of the Fountain Inn, located on the west side of Queen Street north of Vine Street. (Opened by Christopher Reigart in 1758.)

as conservatives declared, "the laws and the constitution are being replaced by the resolves of the people. It is the beginning of Republicanism."

On July 9 hundreds of enthusiastic patriots gathered at the Lancaster Court House to chose representatives. Matthias Slough, William Atlee, Alexander Lowrey and George Ross were among the eight delegates elected to attend the Philadelphia Convention. The Lancaster group, zealous patriots, were ready to support plans for decisive action. When they attended the colony-wide Convention on July 15, they agreed to a resolution that Pennsylvania should send a delegation to the Continental Congress and accepted the proposition that the colony should be morally bound to abide by the decisions Congress reached, especially in the case of a proposed boycott of all imported goods.

A committee of the Convention remained in Philadelphia to present the resolutions to the Assembly. Apparently the delegates swarmed into the State House, lobbying and pressuring the assemblymen. The popular clamor was so great that the Assembly accepted the recommendation of the Convention to send delegates to the First Continental Congress. George Ross of Lancaster was among the seven men chosen.

The First Continental Congress, which met in early September, constituted a great milestone in the creation of a union of the thirteen colonies. Its most immediate accomplishment, however, was a national non-importation agreement, whereby no British goods were to be imported into America. Throughout the fall session, Ross lent his full and complete support to this agreement and to the organization of patriots into Committees of Inspection and Observation to enforce the boycotts.

Lancaster patriots responded by establishing a county-wide committee that included seventy-seven people organized into divisions within the county. The Committee operated with perfect vigilance, keeping the county free from British products. In Lancaster it was the news of the Lexington and Concord battles, fought on April 19, 1775, that brought its citizens to a general denunciation of the British and to a decision that the British had to be resisted by force.

In Lancaster two militia companies were organized immediately and by August 1775 were in Massachusetts, ready to join in the siege of Boston. Throughout the fall and winter months additional military units organized, drilled and waited for their marching orders. There was, in spite of military preparation, little talk of actual separation from England. Jasper Yeates, for example, thought that union with Great Britain was essential to the safety and health of America. "Our present glorious struggle," he said, "is for the preservation of our privileges, not for an Independence."

That attitude which was generally reflected in the thinking of most patriots in Lancaster changed in the early months of 1776. It changed for several reasons: (1) the actual fighting, taking place in New England in the fall and the bloody siege of Quebec on New Year's eve, engendered hatred toward Great Britain. The brutality of the fighting shocked many Americans. (2) The January publication of Thomas Paine's *Common Sense,* widely read in Lancaster, convinced many Lancastrians of the need for political independence. Paine's work was a brilliant synthesis attacking the entire concept of monarchy and describing the advantages of independence. Within a few weeks over a hundred thousand copies circulated throughout the state and thousands in Lancaster County. It was on the minds of most people. It brought around many people who had hitherto been unenthusiastic about independence. Some, of course, reacted as violently in the opposite direction. Lancaster's patriot leaders, led by George Ross, warmly espoused the independence drive.

When news of the Declaration of Independence arrived in Lancaster on July 7, 1776, a continual round of celebrations began. One by one legal officers of the Crown flocked to the court house and surrendered their commissions. The justices of the peace, judges of the courts and other public officials suspended business, refusing to recognize the King. In symbolic protest the English coat of arms was removed from the court house. It would, however, take a lengthy and costly war to ensure that the coat of arms would remain permanently removed.

A Time For Leadership

After April 1775 there was no doubt that the revolutionary party controlled the politics of Lancaster county and provided the necessary leadership to make it safe for the patriot cause. Although a number of younger faces were later added to the leadership roster, power remained lodged within the coterie of men who had led the opposition to Parliamentary and Crown policies before 1775.

Locally, patriot activities were carried out by a Committee of Safety, in part comprised of Edward Shippen, Jasper Yeates, William Atlee, Charles Hall, Casper Schaffner and Adam Reigart. This committee was essentially a civilian body, however, which complied with directives from the State Committee of Safety and the Continental Congress. It assumed the initial responsibility for raising and equipping companies of soldiers. That task was relatively easy because the strength of the patriot cause was so great that enlistments were heavy throughout the war, with perhaps close to 50% of those eligible having seen some service by the end of the fighting. Most of the county's political leaders eventually helped form companies and were often chosen as high ranking officers.

The committee also had the awesome responsibility of maintaining peace and order in the county. Though not one battle was fought within the boundaries of the county, large numbers of militiamen and prisoners of war were quartered there. Each imposed a different sort of challenge. Often the militia, largely undisciplined farm boys and villagers, was unruly; fights, disturbances and riots were common, especially in Lancaster Borough and particularly in the 1775–1777 period. The Safety Committee's justice, however, was swift and without appeal. Hundreds of men were fined, jailed and physically punished for these infractions. Occasionally, troops refused to obey marching orders or simply deserted; they, too, were imprisoned. Sometimes, as was the case in January 1777, soldiers would desert their posts outside of the county. In this instance an impressive number of Lancaster soldiers fled the Philadelphia area and returned to Lancaster, much to the dismay and embarrassment of patriot officials.

At various times thousands of British prisoners were confined to temporary or permanent barracks in the county. These unfortunates included officers and regulars of the British army, German mercenaries, called Hessians, and some political prisoners and their wards and relatives. In 1781, for example, the borough bulged with 1,400 military and political prisoners, plus about 600 women and children. Sickness and disease were commonplace amidst such crowded conditions. The Safety Committee and the Prison Commissary were responsible for their care. This required finding local merchants to supply the needed rations and medical attention. More than once the overcrowding resulted in the furloughing of prisoners into private homes where they worked for farmers, merchants and craftsmen. In March 1777 a large number of Hessian prisoners were placed throughout the county in this manner by the Safety Committee.

Sometimes the prisoners in the borough became violent, as was the case on June 4, 1777. Late that evening a group of prisoners seized the guards, took away their firearms and beat them with clubs—in

The Pennsylvania stretcher table found in smaller rooms of public houses lent itself to gaming, eating, drinking, and talking. The four stretchers at the bottom added great stability to the table and provided elevation of the patrons' feet from the draughty floor.

preparation for an escape attempt. An alert sentry rang the alarm bell, and the militia arrived on the scene to suppress the break-out. The Safety Committee appeared at the barracks and gave overall direction to the militia and ensured that the borough's residents were safe from harm. Many of the guardsmen were elderly or suffered from infirmities that prevented them from joining the militia. This situation added to the burden of the political leadership, requiring additional, continual attention. Often committee members actually commanded, though temporarily, the guard units themselves. The guard units, under the direction of the committee, also protected the ammunition and storehouses, at least while the militia companies were out of the county.

War provisions were always in short supply. The committee was charged with the duty of obtaining muskets, bayonets, lead, shot, powder and other materials used in combat. That meant locating the gunmakers and finding the workmen. Local craftsmen complained that the government did not pay them sufficiently for their endeavors. Jasper Yeates, the committee's chairman in 1776, wrote to the state Committee of Safety explaining that Lancaster's workers could not possibly continue to manufacture guns at the current rate of pay. The problem remained, however, and the committee was forced eventually to plead and arm-twist to get contracts fulfilled.

Wagons, horses, blankets, clothing, shoes and foodstuffs of all kinds were also high priority war items. Lancaster was a major supplier, and the Safety Committee negotiated the contracts with local farmers, craftsmen and workers. Some contracts were made public. Advertisements were posted around the county announcing the condition of contract. In April 1777 an advertisement read,

> Some hundreds of waggons [sic], with four horses and a driver to each, are immediately wanted for this service to whom we [Safety Committee] are directed to mention, that thirty shillings per day will be given, from the day they leave their respective homes, until they return to the same, while in service, allowing time for coming and going.

If products could not be obtained by voluntary means, the committee simply seized what it needed, either leaving a promissory note or paying the amount authorized by the State Safety Committee. Most products taken under these circumstances were those in short supply which brought higher prices in the public market than the government was prepared to pay.

Local committees were expected to implement legal orders and regulations approved by state and continental officials. The range of activities that engaged the time and energy of the committees was wide. One such important order concerned the use of continental currency. Apparently some merchants refused to accept the currency or wanted higher prices than that allowed by the Continental Congress. Local committees were empowered to close the shops, stores and warehouses of non-compliers. Should a merchant be found guilty as a first offender, he was "to be considered a dangerous member of society and forfeit the goods offered for sale or bargained for or debt contracted." Forgers, counterfeiters and even murders fell under the temporary jurisdiction of the Safety Committee.

A Leadership Profile

"I have known four and twenty leaders of revolt," sang Robert Browning, but this book deals primarily with just twelve. These men played the leading roles in determining the course of the Revolution in Lancaster County. Most of them also provided leadership in colony-wide affairs (later state-wide), and a few of them were national figures, men whose stature certainly ranked them far below such notables as Benjamin Franklin, George Washington, John Adams and Thomas Jefferson, but who nonetheless made substantial contributions and who frequently interacted with the Revolution's great leaders.

Generally, however, these twelve—William Atlee, William Bausman, Charles Hall, William Henry, John Hubley, Alexander Lowrey, Adam Reigart, George Ross, Casper Schaffner, Edward Shippen, Matthias Slough and Jasper Yeates—worked locally to organize the county politically and drive the mass of citizenry to support the Revolution. They were the Revolution's popular leaders, even though by background and economic status they now constituted something of an elite group themselves.

Ideological bonds held the twelve together. They were genuinely dedicated to the Revolution, based on their belief in republican institutions. In this sense they recognized the superiority of republicanism, although as late as 1775 they continued to pay homage to the person of King George III. Most of them were consumed by a passion to preserve their way of life and were correspondingly conservative in their views of society. When they demanded their rights as Englishmen, they were expressing this conservative bent.

As a group, the twelve were surprisingly young, averaging around 35 years old, if one excludes Edward Shippen, who at 72 was the senior revolutionary. John Hubley at 28 and Jasper Yeates at 30 were the youngest with the remainder between 33 and 48. With one exception, none were in their 50's or 60's. Although an age gap of two generations stood between the eldest and the youngest, the accent was definitely on youth.

Of the twelve, ten were wealthy men of substance and property; the other two, Charles Hall, a silversmith, and Casper Schaffner, a wool dyer, were by no means men of unsubstantial wealth. Several, Alexander Lowrey, George Ross, William Henry, Edward Shippen and William Bausman, could be considered landed gentry, at least in terms of the size of their respective holdings. Three, William Bausman, Adam Reigart and Matthias Slough, were men of commerce, owning taverns and engaging in the buying and selling of foodstuffs and other provisions. Five, Jasper Yeates, William Atlee, John Hubley, George Ross and Edward Shippen, were trained in the law; and, though two of them branched out into other activities, they practiced law as their profession on a full time basis. Only William Henry stood alone. An inventor and skilled craftsman, his work was known and appreciated throughout the colonies, particularly his fame as a gunmaker.

Slave-owning was not ubiquitous in the county, but at least five of the twelve held slaves. None were what could be called extensive holders; nor were slaves economically important to them. Slough and Ross owned three, Lowrey two, and Hubley and Yeates one each. In 1780 there were approximately 807 slaves in the county, but by 1800 the state's gradual emancipation law and voluntary manumission reduced the number to less than 200. The attitude of Lancaster's Revolutionary leaders towards slavery was less an indication of the importance of the institution, either socially or economically, and more a product of the times. All, therefore, seemed to have been able to avoid a direct confrontation on a subject that did not intimately relate to their social position in the community or to their livelihood.

Ethnically, the twelve came from widely varied backgrounds. Five were from German stock, four were English and three had Scotch backgrounds. While eleven of them were born in the American colonies, only Irish-born Alexander Lowrey was a non-native. Interestingly, just five were born in Lancaster county, most of the others arriving with their parents during early childhood or adolescence.

Their religious backgrounds illustrate a further pluralism. Apparently all were regular church-goers, thus escaping the Enlightenment tradition of Deism and religious cynicism, if not actual contempt. At least one, Henry, was able to move from one denomination to another with some ease, but the rest showed a high degree of denominational consistency. Of the twelve, four were Episcopalian, three Presbyterian, three Lutheran, and two German Reformed. No Catholic or Jew was numbered among their ranks. They seemed, despite regular church attendance, to be a worldly group, fully enjoying the fruits of their wealth and eschewing the asceticism of New England Calvinism.

As the Revolution progressed and as bloodshed increased all around them, they retained a sense of legality and moderation in their actions. This was still a violent time when the whip, pillory and stocks, and rough treatment were common; but they provided responsible, moderate leadership and lacked the vindictiveness that would be associated with the French Revolution a decade or so later. At one point in the summer of 1775, they tried to prevent the more zealous among their ranks from intimidating and assaulting the pacifist-minded Mennonites, insisting that "no one . . . be molested or prejudiced because of his conscientious persuasion or practice, nor be compelled to do or suffer anything contrary to his religious persuasion." In a phrase, they were uncommonly fair-minded men.

Although the twelve showed no tendency to mobbism, they had a healthy respect for public opinion. They were unusually quick to hold a public meeting or call a county convention; they viewed themselves as the county's popular leaders and most would support the reduced suffrage qualifications contained in the state's first constitution in 1776. The obvious exception was Ross, who opposed the final draft because he regarded it as too democratic. They desired intercourse between themselves and those whom they led. Yet, that did not prevent them from meeting secretly to plot the destiny of the Revolution in the county. That was consistent with their leadership values. It was consistent because this was an age in which the common man deferred to his social and economic betters, where such an elite could rule. Lancaster was very much a frontier community, the borough a place of 3,000 hardy souls, the outlying villages no more than cross roads where a few farmhouses stood. The twelve constituted something of a meritocracy, rising on their own talents, although by 1775 they were at the top of the social and economic ladder and expected to rule.

A large majority of the twelve saw military service, albeit for most it was brief duty. As befitted their standing in the community, they were chosen officers in local military units. Lowrey, Slough and Ross became colonels, while Hubley and Schaffner served as majors. Their importance in military matters, however, was not generally in winning battlefield decoration but in the areas of supply, military contracting and procurement. Slough used his merchant connections to become one of the county's largest suppliers of war provisions. Atlee ran the prison system in the county. Hubley served as supply commissary and built the powder magazine in the borough. Lowrey was a procurement agent, hired to supply clothing and blankets. Ross was an inspector of military stores. Hall commanded Lancaster's military storehouse. Reigart provided valuable agricultural foodstuffs. Lastly, Henry made guns, was a procurement agent and served as an assistant commissary officer in the county. In summary, these men of influence and means were able to use their business and commercial connections to great advantage. Their true worth must be measured by a sense of dedication to public service that characterized Revolutionary leadership everywhere.

TWELVE WHO LED A
REVOLUTION

William A. Atlee: Attorney

The American Revolution brought challenges of a different and demanding sort to many patriots, and not the least to William Atlee, a Lancaster lawyer who became the borough's chief Burgess (Mayor), chairman of the county's Committee of Safety, and the State's commissary of the prison system in Lancaster.

Atlee was Burgess during the New England crisis period when the British closed Boston harbor and curtailed several of the colonial rights of Massachusetts' citizens. He took the lead in forming Lancaster's Committee of Correspondence, which was charged with the responsibility of maintaining close communications with other colonies and monitoring the Massachusetts situation.

By July 1774 patriots throughout Pennsylvania were urging the General Assembly to send delegates to the proposed Continental Congress. A special state-wide convention, called to pressure the assembly, was held, and Atlee was one of Lancaster's representatives. The convention adopted a set of "instructions" stating the colonists' determination to preserve their liberty and rejecting Parliamentary supremacy over them. Atlee served as a member of the "instruction" sub-committee, which later drafted regulations dictating the actions of Pennsylvania's delegates to the First Continental Congress.

In 1776 he was chosen chairman of the local Public Safety Committee. This assignment required him to perform a variety of duties: protecting the county from attack; purchasing supplies and equipment for military use, sometimes confiscating them; and enforcing the rules and orders of the state committee of Public Safety. The evacuation of supplies out of Philadelphia, prior to the British invasion, was accomplished with wagons procured under Atlee's direction.

During the years 1777 and 1778 he served as prison commissary. A substantial number of political and military prisoners were confined in Lancaster County, including not only regular prisoners but, in some cases, the wards and relatives of prisoners as well. As prison commissary, he had extensive duties involving the care of high-level prisoners, travel arrangements and transfer of war captives, repair and upkeep of the prisoner barracks and some responsibility for the security of the local residents.

His ardent patriot convictions plus his fine legal mind earned him appointment to the Supreme Court of Pennsylvania, and he was reappointed in 1784. He rounded out his career with a subsequent appointment as President Judge of the district comprising Chester, Lancaster, Dauphin and York counties. He died in 1793.

William Bausman: Merchant

Innkeeper, merchant and landowner, William Bausman joined the patriot cause very early in the struggle against Great Britian. A resident of Lancaster Borough, he was a member of its Committee of Correspondence and later served on the Committee of Observation and Inspection. Prior to the actual fighting, he was especially active in pursuing violators of the patriot boycotts. A merchant who engaged in substantial trade, Bausman scrupulously obeyed the import prohibitions, refusing to traffic in banned items, and he was prepared to stop all those who violated the boycott.

In the crucial period, 1774–1777, he was Chief Burgess of the borough, at a time when the town was inundated with exiles, refugees, prisoners and militiamen. He took on a new assignment in 1777, becoming a special State Commissioner responsible for the disposition of the estates of those defined as traitors by the State Council of Safety.

As a merchant and innkeeper, Bausman was in a special position to help the Continental Army. Throughout the war he held contracts with State and Continental officials providing badly needed supplies. He specialized in providing beef and lamb products.

For a brief period he was barracks master of the borough's prisoner of war facility, and worked closely with other patriots in maintaining

The sign of the County House, located on King Street east of Duke Street. (In 1745 this inn was kept by William Bausman.)

order in the borough. In addition to these peculiarly war-time posts, he was for short periods County Commissioner, Recorder of Deeds and Justice of the Peace.

Charles Hall: Silversmith

Though Charles Hall never really earned a colony-wide reputation, he was, nonetheless, a tireless devotee to the revolutionary cause. Locally he assumed many significant responsibilities. Trained as a silversmith and goldsmith, and an occasional watchmaker, Hall moved to Lancaster from Philadelphia while just a young man. He was one of the few skilled craftsmen to assume a leadership position in the county.

Hall was a member of both the Committee of Correspondence and the Committee of Observation, the first two revolutionary committees established in Lancaster. Once the fighting commenced, however, he joined the local militia, enlisting in Captain Samuel Boyd's company. Only 34, Hall was expected to fulfill his military obligation. He was sent to New Jersey during the summer of 1776 where he earned a promotion from lieutenant to captain, returning to Lancaster in February 1777.

Hall spent the latter part of the war as a state agent, involved in the seizing of the estates of British sympathizers convicted of treason. A fair number of such "tainted traitors" were convicted and their properties sold at public auction. The monies were transferred from Hall to the State Treasury.

At the very end of the war, Hall was given command of the military storehouse, an assignment that placed all government supplies under his care. He also performed some duties relative to the prison system, probably as a guard.

One of his last civic contributions was his participation in the founding of a boys' academy in Lancaster Borough in 1780, a school which became Franklin College. Hall died unexpectedly in 1783.

William Henry: Inventor and Gunsmith

William Henry is best known as one of the county's leading inventors, who also ran a large gun-factory. In this latter capacity he was employed by the province of Pennsylvania to manufacture and repair arms for the militia. The work was considered so essential to the colonial cause that his workmen were exempted from military service.

During the war, Henry held a number of governmental offices, including justice of the peace, member of the Pennsylvania Assembly, and member of the Safety Council of Pennsylvania. He also served as Treasurer of Lancaster County from 1777 to 1785 and held control of the county's finances during a critical period of the American Revolution.

Perhaps his greatest value to the patriot cause came as a procurement officer for the Continental Army. At the onset of the war, he was appointed Assistant Commissary General for Lancaster, and placed extensive orders for provisions among farmers and merchants. Henry's extensive knowledge of Lancaster County made his selection an invaluable one, and letters from George Washington, Horatio Gates, Harry "Lighthorse" Lee and Benjamin Stoddart indicate that he discharged this responsibility with considerable success.

The demands on Henry were also somewhat unusual socially. Fearful of capture or of living under British rule, many Philadelphians moved temporarily to Lancaster. Henry's office, located on Penn Square just north of old City Hall, was a favorite rendezvous for those displaced, a spot to discuss the latest news or just to socialize. His private residence became something of a resort where famous evacuated persons spent a leisurely exile, especially those of culture and intellect. David Rittenhouse, John Hart and Thomas Paine were among Henry's most notable guests.

John Hubley: Attorney

The Hubleys were among the most powerful and well respected German families in Lancaster County and deeply committed to the patriot cause. John Hubley's Uncle Bernard was particularly active, serving as Assistant Burgess of Lancaster Borough in 1750, 1757, 1766 and 1767. He also served several terms as a County Commissioner. Bernard made his fortune in the tanning and farming businesses. His brother Michael, John's father, was a justice of the peace in the county, exerting considerable political influence. During the war he was for a time the barrack-master of the county installation.

John was trained as a lawyer, reading law, as many bright and well-off young men did, with Edward Shippen. His first major revolutionary assignment was to the State Committee of Safety in 1776, an appointment which brought quickly a number of auxiliary responsibilities. Principal among them was the task of maintaining the supplies of the continental and state militias in Lancaster, earning him the title of Commissary with the rank of major. He was then ordered by the Safety Committee to locate cobblers among the Hessian prisoners quartered in Lancaster and to compel them to produce shoes for the state.

In February 1777 he was assigned the crucial task of constructing a powder magazine in the borough. This was completed rapidly and became especially significant following the British capture of Philadelphia.

In addition to these specific military assignments, he held several political positions. In 1776 he was one of Lancaster's delegates to the State Constitutional Convention and voted, as a member of the state ratification convention, to approve the Federal Constitution in 1787. From the 1770's to the 1790's he was variously Prothonotary, Clerk of the Orphan's Court, Clerk of Quarter Sessions and Recorder of Deeds. He died in 1821 at the age of 74.

Alexander Lowrey: Fur Trader

Irish-born Alexander Lowrey arrived in America in 1729, settling in Donegal Township. By profession he was a fur trader and spent a considerable amount of time among the Indians. He made numerous trips into the northwest and Mississippi Valley regions, earning the confidence of many tribes beyond the Appalachian Mountains.

Lowrey accumulated a substantial fortune in the fur trade business and, after 1755, began to purchase large tracts of land in the county, although he remained in the fur trade with his sons and a partner for the next 40 years.

As the war approached, Lowrey became active in behalf of the patriot cause. He was placed on the first Committee of Correspondence in July 1774. By December 1774 the local patriots had formed a committee to observe the activities of suspected British sympathizers and to prevent the consumption of British tea, then the object of a patriot boycott. Lowrey served zealously, vigorously pursuing all leads.

In July 1775, as a delegate from Lancaster, he went to the colony-wide convention, which pressured the General Assembly into sending representatives to the First Continental Congress. When elected to the Assembly itself several months later, beginning a tenure that exceeded a decade, he steadfastly supported patriot proposals.

Utterly destitute of clothing and uniforms in the winter of 1777, the Continental Army hired agents to procure blankets from virtually any

Though the slant-sided shape was the most common for the sturdy pewter mugs and tankards found in the early inn, the more elegant tulip-shape was frequently provided by domestic pewterers.

available source. With his wide trading contacts, Lowrey's selection as an agent proved to be a particularly wise choice.

As did many political leaders, Lowrey served in the militia. He commanded the third battalion of the Lancaster militia and, as a full colonel, led his command at the Battle of Brandywine. Following the war, he retired to his family farm near Marietta and held a final post as Justice of the Peace before his death in 1806.

Adam Reigart: Tavern Keeper

Adam Reigart was best known as the proprietor of the Grape Tavern, a hostelry that became the general headquarters of Lancaster's patriots. Patriots chose his place to hold their meetings, plan strategy and communicate with other revolutionary sympathizers. The Grape was used extensively by the Committees of Observation and Safety, especially during the early years of the Revolution. He also owned other taverns which were communication and organization centers.

A true revolutionary agitator, Reigart was among the most vociferous and radical among Lancaster's political leaders. During those years before the colonists took up arms against the British, when the Parliament imposed its taxation policies in the colonies, he took the lead in fomenting local opposition. The incipient revolutionaries often met privately in his home; only later, after the fighting commenced, did the new, more formal committees move their operations to the Grape Tavern.

His most important political responsibility was as a member of the Safety Committee. Reigart, however, eventually joined the colonial militia, with the rank of Lieutenant Colonel, and served under his close friend and confident, General Edward Hand.

An owner of several farms, he personally supplied large quantities of agricultural produce to the militia. Apparently, he suffered substantial financial loss in the process, because he was not compensated for some of the supplies.

Toward the end of the Revolution, Reigart was elected to the state legislature, was active in the formation of Franklin Academy and became a member of its first Board of Trustees in 1787.

George Ross: Attorney

There is no question that George Ross was Lancaster's preeminent political leader, whose reputation carried to the far ends of Britain's North American colonies. Born in New Castle, Delaware in 1730 he

The red clay of parts of southeastern Pennsylvania yielded material for stout drinking and pouring vessels, which in the Lancaster area were sometimes ornamented brightly with slip and sgraffito decorations.

was educated in Philadelphia, studied law and moved to Lancaster in 1751, where he commenced his public career.

For a decade and a half he remained engaged in his legal practice, entering the political arena in 1768 as an assemblyman. Throughout the next 10 years in the colonial assembly, he earned the confidence and approbation of colony-wide leaders. Consequently, Ross was chosen by the Assembly to be a delegate to both the First and Second Continental Congresses. Interestingly enough, his support of vigorous and bold action against the British following the Boston Port Bill, along with that of other leaders from the central part of the colony, was a major factor in Pennsylvania's commitment to the defense of Boston and decisive in moving the assembly to send delegates to the Continental Congress. In his capacity as a delegate to the Second Continental Congress, Ross became a signer of the Declaration of Independence. Ross's national positions brought him into contact with Benjamin Franklin, George Washington, Thomas Jefferson, John Adams and other luminaries of the day.

Locally, he served on the county revolutionary committees and gave direction to Lancaster's revolutionary activities. Ross also found time to organize a company of militia in 1775 and to preside at a large military convention one year later, which chose brigadier generals for the associated battalions.

Furthermore, he was called to render additional service for the colony. In 1775 he joined the Committee of Safety with responsibilities as an inspector of military stores. He also provided important service as a member of the State Constitutional Convention of 1776 and was chosen its vice-president, although he did not support the final product.

His final appointment was to the bench of the Admiralty Court in March 1779, but he died suddenly in July of the same year. He was only 49.

Casper Schaffner: Merchant

One of the most unnoticed and least recognized of Lancaster's revolutionaries was Casper Schaffner (also spelled Shaffner) who was a member of one of Lancaster's most prominent 18th century families. Schaffner's importance comes not from battlefield heroics or statesmanship at a high level but because he represented an important element in the Revolutionary War: the progressive, forward-looking first and second generation Americans of German descent who supported devotedly the patriot cause. His support disproves the opinion of those who believe that most upperclass Germans in Lancaster opposed the Revolution. Schaffner was a leader among a large element which actively backed the war against the British.

Schaffner was born in Lancaster in 1737. His father was by profession a "blue dyer." He used a process of employing indigo to achieve a deep purple-blue color which had remarkable holding powers for dyes of that time. Young Casper joined his father in business.

Schaffner's first activity on behalf of the patriot cause was his membership on the Committee of Observation and Inspection in December 1774. This committee was the vanguard of opposition to British policies and included the leaders selected by the patriots to shepherd the community through difficult times. Schaffner was one of the committee members present at the May 1, 1775 Grape Tavern meeting when the fateful decision was made to take up arms against the English. He lent his full support to the decision. When the local war effort was assigned to the Committee of Safety, Schaffner was elected to Lancaster's first committee.

Schaffner, 40 years of age, did not join the fighting, but he had two younger brothers who fought. His youngest brother George at age 20 was a member of Col. Sam Atlee's regiment and eventually became a major. His brother Peter also served with distinction. At home Casper served as a guard for prisoners in Lancaster.

Schaffner served several terms as assistant borough clerk in Lancaster between 1760 and 1767 and is listed as clerk in 1774 and every year from 1788 to 1796. He also served as Burgess for several years and was a County Commissioner in 1787.

In 1780 Schaffner, with several other leading citizens (Jasper Yeates, George Ross and Charles Hall), hired a teacher to operate an academy for their sons. They believed that the local schools were incapable of teaching more advanced subjects. This first academy led eventually to the founding of Franklin College. Casper Schaffner was a member of its first board of trustees.

Edward Shippen: Attorney

Trained in Latin, French and Greek, Edward Shippen seemed an unlikely revolutionary. By 1775 he was in his 70's and had lived for many years in Philadelphia where he had been a Judge, Prothonotary, Council member and Mayor.

In Lancaster, his home in his latter years, Shippen soon became an elder statesman and served as both a participant and advisor to the patriots. His support gave the Revolution respectability. He was usually made the "honorary chairman" of the revolutionary committees, though when aroused, as in the Boston relief fund, he could be a tiger. He was the nominal chairman of the Committee of Correspondence, but George Ross was the Committee's real leader.

Shippen held most of the county offices including Prothonotary, Register of Wills and Recorder of Deeds, and for a number of years he was Chief Burgess of the borough of Lancaster—a position he was serving in when the famous Paxton massacre occurred.

Ironically, Shippen's son Edward Shippen, Jr., who lived in Philadelphia, was not a patriot and during the British occupation of Philadelphia socialized with and befriended British officers. The younger Shippen's daughter Peggy ultimately married the traitor Benedict Arnold. None of those events, however, deterred the elder Shippen's revolutionary zeal and determination. Unfortunately he died in 1781 and did not live to witness the conclusion of the war.

Matthias Slough: Merchant

One of Lancaster Borough's most prominent and visible revolutionaries was Matthias Slough. Matthias was about 13 years old when his father brought him to Lancaster in 1747; and, while still very young, he became the owner of the White Swan Inn, a popular tavern located where the Watt and Shand store now stands. Slough, however, soon branched out into other mercantile fields and engaged in a variety of commercial activities.

As an early opponent of British policies toward the colonies, he was a member of the local patriot Committee of Correspondence. His tavern was a favorite meeting place of German colonists, who eagerly exchanged the most recent news of rapidly unfolding events.

Following Lexington and Concord, Slough placed a large store of lead and powder at the disposal of the Revolutionary forces. Throughout the war he supplied the Continental Army with provisions and materials. At one point in December 1775, when several hundred British prisoners in Lancaster went unfed, he supplied emergency rations to them, a responsibility he continued on a more regular basis.

The Lancaster tavernkeeper also had a short military career. He served briefly in the militia as Colonel of the Seventh Lancaster County Battalion. Though his most outstanding contributions were

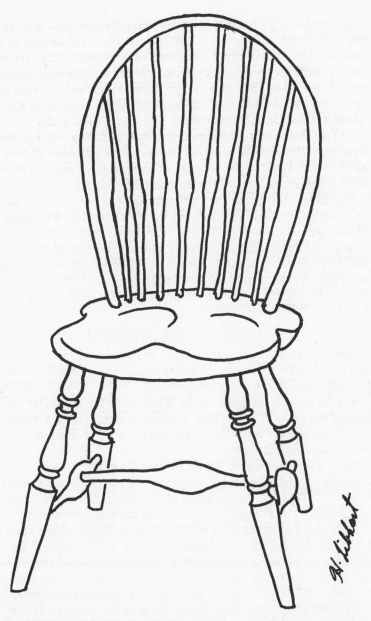

Adapted from a more formal English prototype, the American Windsor (or "hoop and stick") was common both in homes and in public houses, and was notable for its strength, comfort, and lightness.

not military in nature, his unit did take part in the battle of Long Island in August 1776.

He returned from military duty and to his merchant-revolutionary activities. The Continental Congress let numerous contracts with merchants, and Slough was a regular purveyor of clothing, shoes, blankets, gun powder and other military provisions.

Like many gentlemen of standing and wealth, he was expected to provide governmental leadership. Slough was elected to the colonial and state assemblies of 1774, 1775, 1777, 1780 and 1783, where he toiled for the patriot cause. He participated in the state convention, which met in July 1774, and urged the state Assembly to send delegates to the First Continental Congress.

Following the war he was involved in a number of civic and business ventures. In 1793 he became one of the five superintendents of the Philadelphia and Lancaster Turnpike, with responsibilities for the construction of the last fifth of the road—that section nearest to Lancaster. Slough then turned his attention to the operation of stagecoach lines between Lancaster and Philadelphia, later adding a line from Lancaster to Shippensburg.

Jasper Yeates: Attorney

Jasper Yeates, barely 30 years old when the American Revolution broke out, assumed an important role in the patriot struggle. Ironically, Yeates was a relative newcomer to the county, emigrating in the late 1760's from Philadelphia, where he had pursued his formal schooling and was admitted to the practice of law. In just a few years he established himself as the preeminent legal mind of the central region of the colony and developed an extensive practice.

Yeates was a moving force behind the initial opposition to British policies following the British Port Bill. He was in the central cadre of local patriots that gave direction to the Revolution in Lancaster. As a member of the general Committee of Correspondence, and later, as a member of the Committee of Observation and Inspection, he had a direct responsibility in the enforcement of boycotts and other policies of the Continental Congress.

It was, however, as chairman of the Committee of Safety that Yeates made his most individual contribution. Following the outbreak of fighting, Committees of Safety were organized in each county, for the purpose of providing temporary governmental and political leadership. These committees did the lion's share of the military recruitment, collected arms and war supplies and were responsible for the safety of their counties. To Yeates fell the difficult task of organizing Lancaster's early war effort.

After the war, Yeates returned to his legal duties, briefly halting them to serve as one of Lancaster's delegates to the convention that ratified the Federal Constitution in 1787. The culmination of his legal career occurred in 1791 when he was appointed to the bench of the State Supreme Court, a post he held until his death in 1817.

Epilogue

The war with Great Britain ended in 1783, but the challenges raised by independence were just beginning. The military victory had to be translated into a lasting peace and permanent government guaranteed. The Revolution had provided the political leadership with the opportunity to establish these governments both at the state and national level, and thereby give legal form and expression to their political ideals. Yet the process of maintaining them would not be easy.

For Lancaster's political leaders the war's end did not mean a return to "normal" times. The task of serving in peace-time governments and of securing the peace would occupy their attention in the 1780's, culminating in the drafting and ratification of the Constitution of 1787.

LANCASTER'S TWELVE MAJOR REVOLUTIONARY LEADERS

	William Atlee	William Bausman	Charles Hall	William Henry	John Hubley	Alexander Lowrey
Age (in 1775)	40	51	33	46	28	48
National Origin	English	German	English	Scot-French	German	Scotch-Irish
Religion	Episcopalian	German Reformed	Presbyterian	Presbyterian-Moravian	Lutheran	Presbyterian
Principal Occupation	Attorney	Merchant-Innkeeper	Goldsmith Silversmith Watchmaker	Inventor Gunmaker Merchant	Lawyer	Fur Trader
Economic Status	Wealthy	Wealthy	Moderately Wealthy	Wealthy	Moderately Wealthy (though extensive wealth in family)	Wealthy
Place of Birth	Philadelphia	Lancaster	Philadelphia	Chester	Lancaster	Ireland
Slaves Owned	0	0	0	0	1	2

	Adam Reigart	George Ross	Casper Schaffner	Edward Shippen	Matthias Slough	Jasper Yeates
Age (in 1775)	36	45	38	72	42	30
National Origin	German	Scot-Dutch	German	English	German	English
Religion	Lutheran	Episcopalian	German Reformed	Episcopalian	Lutheran	Episcopalian
Principal Occupation	Innkeeper-Merchant	Attorney	Wool dyer	Attorney	Innkeeper-Merchant	Attorney
Economic Status	Wealthy	Wealthy	Moderately Wealthy	Wealthy	Wealthy	Wealthy
Place of Birth	Lancaster	New Castle	Lancaster	Boston	Lancaster	Philadelphia
Slaves Owned	1	3	0	0	3	1

Editor's Note

Dr. G. Terry Madonna is associate professor of American history at Millersville State College where he specalizes in political history. He has published articles on the Jacksonian era and on the present structure of the national Democratic Party. He is also active in practical politics as a party leader and has served as a county commissioner. He recommends for further reading on Lancaster political leadership during the American Revolution the following books: Franklin Ellis and Samuel Evans, *History of Lancaster County, Pennsylvania* (Philadelphia, 1883); *Pennsylvania Colonial Records,* volumes X and XII (Harrisburg, 1838–); Francis Jordan, Jr., *The Life of William Henry* (Lancaster, 1910); Theodore Thayer, *Pennsylvania Politics and the Growth of Democracy, 1740–1776* (Harrisburg, 1953); Robert Brunhouse, *The Counter Revolution in Pennsylvania, 1776–1790* (Harrisburg, 1942).

APPENDIX

COMMITTEE OF CORRESPONDENCE
ESTABLISHED, JUNE 15, 1774

Resolution

And the following Resolves were agreed on at a meeting of the inhabitants of the borough of Lancaster, at the court house in the said borough, on Wednesday, the 15th day of June, 1774: Agreed-that to preserve the Constitutional rights of the inhabitants of America, it is incumbent on every colony, to unite and use the most effectual means to procure a repeal of the late act of Parliament against the town of Boston.

That the act of Parliament for blocking up the port and harbor of Boston, is an invasion of the rights of the inhabitants of the said town, as subjects of the crown of Great Britain. That it is the opinion of the inhabitants at this meeting that the proper and effectual means to be used to obtain a repeal of the said act, will be to put an immediate stop to all imports, and exports, to and from Great Britain, until the same act be repealed.

That the traders and inhabitants of this town will join and concur with the patriotic merchants, manufacturers, tradesmen, and freeholders, of the city and county of Philadelphia, and other parts of this province, in an association or solemn agreement to this purpose, if the same shall be by them thought necessary.

That Edward Shippen, Esq., George Ross, Esq., Jasper Yeates, Esq., Matthias Slough, Esq., James Webb, Esq., William Atlee, Esq., William Henry, Esq., Mr. Ludwig Larman, Mr. William Bausman and Mr. Charles Hall, be a committee to correspond with the general committee of Philadelphia; that these sentiments be immediately forwarded to the committee of correspondence at Philadelphia.

COMMITTEE OF OBSERVATION AND
INSPECTION ESTABLISHED
DECEMBER 15, 1774

Election of Members

On the said 15th day of December, in pursuance to the notice above mentioned, a general election was held at the borough of Lancaster, for this county, and the following persons were chosen as, and for, a committee:

Lancaster borough—Edward Shippen, George Ross, James Webb, Adam Sim. Kuhn, Jasper Yeates, William Atlee, Adam Reigart, Wm. Bausman, Christian Voght, Eberhart Michael, Charles Hall, Casper Schaffner. Conestoga—Martin Bare. Manor—John Killhafer, Jacob Wistler, James Jacks. Hempfield—Val. Breneman. Manheim—Samuel Bear, Sebastian Graff. Paxton—James Burd, Joseph Sherer. Hanover—Timothy Green. Derry—Castle Byers, William Laird, Robert McKee. Londonderry—John Campbell. Paxton—John Bakestose. Upper Paxton—William Patterson. Hanover—William Brown, James Crawford. Mountjoy—James Cunningham, Abrm. Frederick. Rapho—Jacob Erisman, Patrick Hay. Donegal—Bartram Galbraith, Alexander Lowrey, Fred'k Mumma. Warwick—Jacob Erb, Peter Grubb. Lebanon—Thomas Clark, Curtis Grubb, Henry Light. Bethel—Ludwig Shuy, Casper Corr, John Bishon. Heidleburg—John Weiser. Bethel—Killian Long, Sam'l Jones. Elizabeth—Hans Frantz, Lebanon—Henry Bealor. Earl—Alex'r Martin, Emanuel Carpenter, Anthony Ellmaker, Wm. Smith, Zacheus Davis, Geo. Rein, Jno. Brubaker. Cocalico—John Hones. Brecknock—Benj. Lessley. Carnarvon—David Jenkins. Salisbury—James Clemson, Jno. Whitehill. Leacock—David Watson, Nath'l Lightner. Strasburg—Eberhart Grube, Mich'l Witter. Lampeter—Jno. Witmer, Jr. Sadsbury—Robert Baily. Little Britain—John Allton. Drumore—Thos. Porter. Bart—Jacob Bare. Colerain—Joshua Anderson. Martick—Jno. Snodgrass. Drumore—William McEntire. Little Britain—Thomas Whitesides. Bart—Hieronimus Hickman.

COMMITTEE OF OBSERVATION AND
INSPECTION ELECTS EDWARD SHIPPEN CHAIRMAN
AND ENDORSES COLONY-WIDE CONVENTION
JANUARY 14, 1775

Minutes

At a meeting of the committee of inspection of the county of Lancaster, at the Court house, in Lancaster, on Saturday, the 14th day of January, 1775, Edward Shippen, Esq. was chosen chairman.

It was unanimously agreed that in case of any difference in sentiments, the question proposed be determined by the members of committee, voting by townships.

A letter from the committee of correspondence of the City and Liberties of Philadelphia, and another letter from the committee of correspondence of Berks county, were then read; and it being put to vote, whether this committee would appoint deputies to meet the other counties of this province in provincial convention, on Monday, the 23rd January instant, the same was carried in the affirmative:

Yeas; Borough of Lancaster, Hempfield township, Manheim township, Paxton township, Hanover township, Londonderry township, Mountjoy township, Rapho township, Donegal township, Warwick township, Lebanon township, Bethel township, Elizabeth township, Earl township, Brecknock township, Caernarvon township, Salisbury township, Leacock township, Lampeter township, Sadsbury township, Little Britain township, Drumcre township, Colerain township.

Nays; Lancaster township, Derry township, Strasburg township, Bart township.

Absent; Conestoga township, Upper Paxton township, Heidleberg township, Cocalico township, Martick township, Manor township.

The committee then proceeded to appoint deputies, and the following gentlemen, to wit:—Adam Simon Kuhn, James Burd, James Clemson, Esq., Peter Grubb, Sebastian Graff, David Jenkins, and Bartram Galbraith, or any five of them, were nominated to attend the said provincial convention, in behalf of the county of Lancaster.

Edward Shippen, Chairman

LANCASTER PATRIOTS TAKE UP ARMS

Resolve To Resist

The association of the freemen and inhabitants of the county of Lancaster, the 1st May, 1775.

Whereas, the enemies of Great Britain and America have resolved by force of arms to carry into execution the most unjust, tyrannical, and cruel edicts of the British Parliament, and reduce the freeborn sons of America to a state of vassalage, and have flattered themselves, from our unacquaintance with military discipline, that we should become an easy prey to them, or tamely submit and bend our necks to the yoke prepared for us: We do most solemnly agree and associate under the deepest sense of our duty to God, our country, ourselves and posterity, to defend and protect the religious and civil rights of this and our sister colonies, with our lives and fortunes, to the utmost of our abilities, against any power whatsoever that shall attempt to deprive us of them.

And the better to enable us so to do, we will use our utmost diligence to acquaint ourselves with military discipline and the art of war.

We do further agree to divide ourselves into companies not exceeding one hundred men, each, so as to make it most convenient to our situation and settlement, and to elect and choose such persons as the majority of each company shall think proper for officers, viz: for each company a captain, two lieutenants and one ensign, who shall have the power of appointing the other officers under them, necessary for the companies.

That when the companies are formed and the officers chosen and appointed, an association shall be signed by the officers and soldiers of each company, for the good order and government of the officers and soldiers.

LANCASTER PATRIOTS PREPARE FOR WAR

Resolve To Arm

Resolved, that the members of the committee of the county of Lancaster, do, with the utmost expedition, take an account of the number of whites—men, women and children—to the respective townships of this county, and transmit the same to the members of the committee, residing in Lancaster, to be forwarded to the members of the general Congress for the province of Pennsylvania.

Resolved, that the members of the committee do examine the quantity of powder and lead the store-keepers have in their hands, in the respective townships, and that the store-keepers be required that they sell no powder or lead before the first of June next, as they tender the trade and custom of the inhabitants of the respective townships, provided that it be sold only by such store-keepers having a license from two members of the committee.

LOCAL PATRIOTS RAISE MILITARY SUPPLIES

Minutes

At a meeting of the committee of observation, on the 4th day of May, 1775, the Commissioners of the county being also present, Mr. Charles Hamilton agrees, that the county shall have his powder, being 26 casks, at the rate of 14 pounds per cwt. and they paying the carriage; and that the county shall have his lead, being about eight hundred weight, at 45 pence per cwt.

Messrs. Josiah & Robert Lockhart agree that the county shall have their powder, being five quarter casks, at 15 pounds per cwt., they paying the carriage; and their lead at 45 pence per cwt.

Mr. Matthias Slough agrees that the county shall have his powder, being four quarter casks, at 15 pounds per cwt., they paying the carriage; and his lead at 45 pence per cwt.

Mr. Simons by Mr. Levy, Andrew Levy, agrees that the counties shall have his power, being 2 quarter casks, at the rate of 15 pounds per cwt., they paying the carriage; and his lead, being about 200 pounds, at 45 per cwt.

Mr. Christian Wirtz agrees that the county shall have his powder, being 5 quarter casks and some pounds loose, at the rate of 15 pounds per cwt., they paying the carriage; and his lead, being about 150 pounds, at 45 per cwt.

Mr. John Hopson agrees that the county shall have his powder, being 2 quarter casks, at the rate of 15 pounds per cwt., they paying the carriage.

Mr. Crawford agrees that the county shall have his powder, being 10 or 12 pounds, at the rate of 15 pounds per cwt. and carriage.

Mr. Bickham agrees that the county shall have his powder, being 1 quarter cask and some loose powder, at the rate of 15 pounds per cwt. and carriage; and his lead at 45 per cwt.

Mr. Graff agrees that the county shall have his powder, being about a quarter cask, at the rate of 15 pounds per cwt. paying carriage.

LANCASTER BICENTENNIAL COMMITTEE, INC.

Donald G. Goldstrom, *Chairman*

Lancaster County
in the
American Revolution

The official Bicentennial Book series is published by the Lancaster County Bicentennial Committee in an effort to preserve the rich heritage of the greater Lancaster area during the American Revolution. Seven books are planned for the series, each revealing a different aspect of the County's participation.

BOOKS IN SERIES

A WAY OF LIFE by Jim Kinter with illustrations by Michael Abel.

While the Lancaster area was not the site of any military engagements in the Revolution, its men saw action from Boston to Yorktowne. The area played the important role of supplying war materiel and served as a training ground for troops and campsite for prisoners and wounded.

1974 64pp. 5½ × 8½ L.C. 74–29188 ISBN 0–915010–04–6 paper $2.00

THE PENNSYLVANIA RIFLE by Samuel E. Dyke with illustrations by Constantine Kermes.

The history of the Pennsylvania–Kentucky Rifle is traced from the hunting rifle of the German settlers, to the Lancaster County gunsmiths, to their ultimate use in the American Revolution by the Continental Army.

1974 64pp. 5½ × 8½ L.C. 74–29189 ISBN 0–915010–05–4 paper $2.00

FIGHTING THE BATTLES: LANCASTER'S SOLDIERS MARCH OFF TO WAR by Frederic Shriver Klein with illustrations by Florence S. Taylor.

Lancaster's riflemen, armed with the famed "Pennsylvania Rifle" from local gunsmiths' shops, quickly established a reputation for marksmanship. Various battles in which Lancastrians participated (all outside the boundaries of Lancaster County) are discussed.

1975 56pp. 5½ × 8½ L.C. 75–15438 ISBN 0–915010–06–2 paper $2.00

THE PERILS OF PATRIOTISM: JOHN JOSEPH HENRY AND THE AMERICAN ATTACK ON QUEBEC, 1775 by J. Samuel Walker with illustrations by Joanne W. Hensel.

An account of the 1775–1776 American Army campaign against Quebec is given as it was seen by a young Lancaster County soldier of seventeen, fighting with Benedict Arnold's forces.

1975 56pp. 5½ × 8½ L.C. 75–15439 ISBN 0–915010–08–9 paper $2.00

THE REVOLUTIONARY LEADERSHIP by G. Terry Madonna
with illustrations by Henry Libhart.

Twelve men worked to insure that battlefield victories would not
be lost in the political arena. This is the story of the committees and
legislatures which met in taverns before and during the American
Revolution to draft and enforce documents of law and to govern the
county and state.

1976 56pp. 5½ × 8½ L.C. 76–8955 ISBN 915010–07–0 paper $2.00

FORTHCOMING TITLES

The Military Marketbasket by John W. W. Loose with illustrations by
Michael Abel.

Prisoners, Pacifists and Loyalists by Rollin C. Steinmetz with illustrations by Grace Steinmetz.

All of the above books as well as the handsome, full-color Bicentennial Calendars may be ordered direct from the co-publisher, post-
paid.

Mail to : SUTTER HOUSE   **ORDER**
         BOX 146   **FORM**
         LITITZ, PA. 17543

Please send me the following Bicentennial Books:

———— copies A WAY OF LIFE by Jim Kinter @ $2.00
———— copies THE PENNSYLVANIA RIFLE by Samuel E. Dyke @ $2.00
———— copies FIGHTING THE BATTLES by Frederic S. Klein @ $2.00
———— copies THE PERILS OF PATRIOTISM by J. S. Walker @ $2.00
———— copies THE REVOLUTIONARY LEADERSHIP by G. Terry
Madonna @ $2.00

Please send me the following Bicentennial Calendars:

———— copies 1976 folded calendar (12 × 18 open) @ $3.00
———— copies 1976 large, non-folding calendar (12 × 18 open). Edition
limited to 5000 copies @ $3.50

I enclose $———— (Pa. residents please add 6% sales tax.)

☐ Please place me on your mailing list for future announcements.

       NAME ————————————————

       ADDRESS ————————————————

————————————————